THE COMMENCEMENT OF SELF

A Poetry Collection

ASIA BATCHELOR

Contents

2

BUDDING

3

SOWED IN TEARS; REAP IN JOY

THE COMMENCEMENT OF SELF

I

Wither, I Will

Predestined

It's true.
It never stops.
Beneath all the layers of "healing"
and "happiness" and "hope."
It's all there.
Inside, as if it were embedded within
your bones at the time of creation.
The hell you fear so much
is here, in you, at every corner you turn.
The darkness always seems to follow.

NEWS FLASH: it's not following you.

Loudest Before The Storm

Sometimes I feel like my mind hates me.
It circles around the same thoughts every day.
Over and over, I am struck by its content .
Drifted off into its sea of torment
I am certain my ship has reached the
ocean floor by now.
And I cannot swim.
Tossed and turned, the waters agonize my body.
I am affected with so much intensity I cannot feel.
My thoughts are all I have.
Yet, they provide no comfort.
They say it is quietest before the storm.
I have never known silence.

Settled

I spend my days lying in the hollow, body-shaped
shadow of my bed.
Surrounded by my comforts,
I roll over to see the midday sun,
shining brightly from the bottom of closed shades.
I startle at the scratchiness of crushed-up pieces
of frosted flakes under my skin,
remembering the dissociative greed of last night's
ritualistic festivities.

In some ways,
I am no different from the dark silhouette I lay upon.
I am nothing but a sheer imitation of life,
of those who have slept on me and stepped on me.
I hold this place in remembrance of my defeat,
of my victory, of my known
and unknown self.

Uniquely made, my silhouette
cannot be duplicated,
and every day it changes just a bit
from repositioning and discomfort.
I despise the changes I must make.

Yet, it is that same discomfort that has caused me
to notice the sun in the first place.

Woe Is Me

And at the end of the day
it is just me alone with my thoughts.
Thoughts that would kill any weaker-minded than me.

Ride

How much longer can I continue on this roller coaster? I never liked rides. The constant up and down, side to side. When I go up, it feels as though I will stay there forever, and sometimes I do. That's the forever that disguises itself as stability. It never lasts. In a blink of an eye and a fall of my soul I am back at the bottom, not where I started but still the bottom nonetheless. It never ends. It never does. I contemplate jumping off, but if I do, where would I land? On the bottom, right? Then I might never experience the top again. It's a lose-lose situation. How did I even get on here? I never got on a line and said, "This is going to be so fun." Heck, I never got a ticket to enter the park. Who placed me on this ride? This ride of delusion has convinced me of permanence at every stage. And though I know it won't last, I don't know that it won't. Oh, delusion. I can live here forever. And I have...or at least I think I have.

Silence

Is my silence not loud enough?
Do my thoughts have to scream at you?
My tongue is immobile,
though it hasn't been in the past.
It grew tired of wiggling when ears stopped listening.
Silence is all I have now.
Though I know it makes no difference either way.

Sad Smiles

Sad smiles shine the brightest in the rooms of the unaware.
Which is them all.
Sad smiles cover the tears of dissatisfaction.
No one will ever know.
Will they?
The smile is so contagious, isn't it?
Infecting everyone but the one behind it.

Clockwork

Precise is the sword
which pierces the hearts of the fallen.
Cut deep; he bleeds and bleeds until
there is no more to pour.
Look down and you will see only one drop,
a speckle on the pavement.

Untitled

You arise from the air.
With a light blow you disappear.
You crumble, you falter.
Is that something to be proud of?
You arise from the bright fire,
standing hot with anger;
anger suppressed in the presence of others.
Fire turns to dust;
dust that salts the eyes of my loved ones;
dust of which will lay on the ground of my grave.
A grave that has had my name on it for ages now.
Not only due to preparation but destruction as well.
Still, I wait.
Wait for the days when I can arise from
my own ashes and sing.
Wait for the days I sing, and someone will listen.
Wait for the days when I listen and understand.
Wait for the day when I, myself am understood.
Until then, I will continue to lie in the depths of my own soul,
lie in the crevices of my own mind,
and lie in the shadows of my demons.
My patience, though, is wearing thin.

Conversation

I yearn for conversation.
I learn from conversation.
I hear the conversations.
In and around,
I hide from conversation.

Regret

I wish upon a star
to erase.
Erase, erase, erase.
Erase until the page is filled
with nothing but smudged lines and marks
and wrinkles and rips.
All in hoes to relieve the letters I can still
see on the page.
So I erase, erase, erase.
It doesn't work; why doesn't it work?
Why can I still see faded letters?
Of the words I wrote by mistake,
that didn't form cohesive sentences,
that didn't produce adequate enough paragraphs.
The paragraphs that will never be read by anyone but me.
I assume.
What's the point of the rubber, anyway?

Sleet

This isn't rain.
It's sleet.
Cutting me piece by piece until all that's left is
the sound of the pellets hitting the floor.
Sleet doesn't grow flowers like rain does.
If only it were raining, maybe then would I see the rosebuds
or even daylilies.
Some sunflowers would be nice.
But sleet...
Sleet slits your eyes, so all you can see is soot.

Bottle

The bottle is empty.
There's no room for filling, either.
The emptiness occupies all the space in the bottle.
Nothing else will fit.
Not a drop of water,
not a trickle of juice,
a bead of sweat,
a glob of blood,
a drizzle of syrup,
or a dribble of tea.

It's funny...
Emptiness is kind of satisfying
when the bottle can never be full.

2

Budding

The Gun

I will use this pain for the development of self,
to give me peace in my future endeavors.
The steady, twisting knife jerking at my heart
will not be comforted by familiar toxicity.
I will continue to bleed until I can pull it from its wedge.
Only then can I say I have moved on.
Only then can I say I am ready for a new knife to appear.
Only then can I say that the clotted blood
will only make it harder
for the next knife to prevail;
even if that knife is wielded by my own hand.
But then, it's never a knife I like to hold.
It's a gun.
A gun that was not given to me
but created out of the suffering of those before me.
Because denying that I had any portion
in its creation somehow takes away
from the pain once the trigger is pulled.
A pain that, though familiar, will never be expected.

Look at the gun in its hole, and tell it the lies you've told me.
The lies I've lived on and with since 2001,
since you first told me you hated me,
since you first felt the tip of the knife piercing

its way through my flesh into my organs.
What now I say,
can you ever do to me that I cannot do to myself?
What pain can be greater?
What suffering can be greater?
None.
None other than the pain I will see you feel once
I am no longer here.
And yes, I said see.
I will see.

Elements

My tears form bright blue rivers that flow into oceans.
I destroy myself,
creating magic from the ashes.
The free flow of self through feeling and time.
I am the fertile soil out of which
grows the prettiest rose.
Light and airy, I blow through the wind
with the ease of a plastic bag.
Just as easily, I am torn apart by the fires
of my mind.
The ashes left behind lay in the soil of my soul,
to create anew.
Here, I stand.
A rose on the battlefield.
Dodging the boots of the unnoticing,
of those unaware of my presence;
unbothered.

I am here, just as the rain falls.
I fill up oceans with madness and
chaos.
Yet, I stand still (firm) in its entirety.
I am what I make me
and I make myself whole.

My Reflection

I'm so proud of you I say as I look in the mirror.
But what about me? she says back to me.
Silence.
We stare into the eyes of another for what feels like hours.
Contrasting every thought in hopes I can regain
a sense of familiarity.
A sense of control.
A sense of self.
Tick tick tick
A glance at the clock reveals only a minute has passed.
What a trick.
She has tricked me yet again.

Faces and Places

I have many faces
in different places.
They all allude to the places I've been before.
Yet, discernment is necessary to understand
just how they have affected me.

I have many faces
in different places.
My expressions are not meant for general consumption.
I walk with my emotional crucifix plastered on my face,
drudging through the pathways I cross.
With plenty of thoughts of minimalism,
I know not where I am headed.
But I know the imminent power
of my destination.

I have many faces
in different places.
Made for the desperation of authenticity.

The Hub

On the journey of healing, I have reached a crossroads. Two paths lay before me, one more rugged and muddy as if walked by the beasts of man, the filthiest of the rich, and those who insist on getting their way. The other, as if fairies with recently cut wings have just discovered those things called feet. Albeit the altruistic artists with respect, and the humblest and wisest of men have gone down such a road. What shall I say while both are so compelling? I am being pulled in either direction. One by revenge, one by love. The two cannot occupy the same space. Yet, I have stood in these woods at this very spot for ages, and I know the beginnings of both, taking only a few steps in either direction and always returning to the point at which I first saw opportunity. How can I progress in both? I shall walk right through, both paths at my side. I have formed an alternate path. Vengeance and care live freely here.

Constancy

The behaviors I know will make me better
fight with the behaviors that have kept me safe.
My mind is a minefield of indecision and anxiety.
I behave as such.
Back and forth,
I run between potential and comfortability.

Paradox

I am a socialite in my heart of hearts
and an introvert in the depths of my anxiety.

3

Sowed In Tears;
Reap In Joy

Oh, Brown Body

Oh, brown body!
You are more than what you deserve.
You are more than what they think of you.
How you love,
what you carry inside.

Oh, brown body!
How delicate and fragile you are.
So easily broken and dismayed.
They will say you're skin and bones.

Oh, brown body!
I've taught you to hide.
To that, I am saddened.
I've taught you to sit and stay.

As I lay a hand on my own shoulder,
pat my own back,
kiss my own forehead,
and stroke my own cheek
in hopes I can undo all the lies I have formerly agreed with.

Oh, brown body!
Learn forgiveness as I have too late.

All Aboard

The mind is akin to a train station. Daily, and all throughout life, trains stop here. These trains carry thoughts. Sometimes every cart of the train stops at the station individually. There are many I have never seen before and even more I have seen multiple times. These are the ones that follow the same route daily, sometimes hourly, sometimes by the minute. These are the trains which I have accepted. These are the trains my mind has become attached to. So, they continue to stop at the station of my mind regularly. Those which I have not seen before come and go but are not accepted. They might even be scheduled to come regularly but I don't remember because I don't pay much mind to them when they stop. If I were to acknowledge these trains and really look into its carts, as I do with the frequent ones, they might begin to come more often and have more influence. A train unaccepted cannot produce real lasting, feeling and sustainability. It is the trains I know which are the basis of my experiences. Accept and explore the new trains, and I might experience thoughts anew.

Self

As I have reached this point again,
I find the only tool necessary for living is love of oneself.
Love and understanding of self, as I know it.
Only to find out that I know nothing about myself.
So vast, so infinite, and so powerful.
I can only fathom a dollop of its entirety.
Oh, self, how you've saved me time and time again.

Nothing To See Here

I know nothing,
but I will learn until I reach
the pinnacle of nothingness.
Ahh, nothingness!

Ode

Ode to the girl hiding behind
the shattered glass of what I
thought would be my womanhood.

Shame I had to shout, stab, cut, and file
her away by any means I knew how.
It's a shame she never got the chance
to present herself in the light of day.
To whom I've shoved deep down
inside the burning flesh I live in
today.
Flesh so worn the pleather on
my boots had a better chance
at convincing the world anew.

I was given opportunity
upon opportunity
upon opportunity
to lift her up from beneath the devil's toes.

Chance upon chance upon chance
to prevent the stench of those same toes
from filling the nostrils of the girl whose nose was too big,
whose head was too small,

whose body was too thin,
whose feet were too long.

Yet, it is those same feet
with which I use to walk in a world so ruthless it is
almost impossible to fathom the possibility
of being any other way;
out from where she is so deeply shoved inside.

Enough

It's enough for me, anyway.
This lonely place is enough;
enough to hold the desires
and appreciation for something outside
myself.
Enough to realize nothing exists there.
I am whole in my loneliness.
The emptiness proves only to show
the mind lacks nothing.
It is that which lacks me.
Here, between me and the space
for all things hoped for
is peace.

A River Fond Of Rocks

I am a river among the trees.
I flow through trees, mud, the underground, dirt
and my favorite: I flow against rocks.
The rocks are my favorite part,
they give me a nice break in the calmness of myself.
They create the beauty of ripples and white water.
Then, I crash back down into the calmness,
making it a little less calm.
I love these rocks,
they've always been there.
Sometimes they move but I know I will encounter
many more as I flow from river to river,
from ocean to ocean.
Oh, these rocks, solid yet ever changing,
I change them just as they change me,
making each other smoother, less sharp and easily portable.
These rocks have shaped my shape and I have shaped it's.
These rocks will forever be my mountains.

This Feeling...

This feeling is way too familiar to go unnoticed, way too familiar to be misunderstood. The halfway point between depressed and ecstatic. Somber. I teeter from each point, usually never surprised at its appearance. But this time. Oh, this time! I am convinced of the diagnosis. The latter end was so captivating I questioned what it ever meant to be sad. I see now I have fooled myself. What is it?

The Renewal Approach

Presently changing and stable,
riding the waves of insanity
in the ocean of spiritual awareness.
In the void between "right"
and "wrong," I emerge
whole.

Here

I have seen the light at the end of the tunnel.
The gleam brings stars into my eyes.
Its glare shines warmth onto my face.
I walk wearily in doubt of its brightness.
The path is feet-ridden and worn.
Here, I recognize those who have come
before me with similar worries.
Still, I must walk.
Despite its intimidation,
I go on.
I go not even of my will.
I go not because others have.
I go because it is necessary.
Because it is the eventual next step.
Because I have stood in the darkness of
the tunnel for far too long.
Because the darkness encompasses chills and strange sounds.
I go where I know I am needed.
And I am needed everywhere outside of here.

Hope

Past the shattered glass,
the curtains open and the light
shines anew.

Author's Note

The poems in this collection remain close to my heart because they symbolize my struggle, rebirth and commencement of self. Now, I won't lie and say I know exactly who I am. Actually, I don't even think it's possible to pinpoint exactly who you are at any given moment. But what I can say is that emotion, isolation and self-contemplation has led me to understand the being I call Asia Krystal Batchelor. These poems are a representation of that. I now realize and appreciate the intense suffering that my mental illnesses caused and still have a tendency to cause me today. Well, because it doesn't stop. I know this is not something anyone wants to hear, but once you have a mental illness there is a very low chance of ever being able to effectively cure it. Mental illness is a chronic sickness of the mind, which is the very place one should find comfort in, within oneself. However, the ability to live with, deal with, love, and find peace within it is doable. I attest to that. I've learned to work around and through my depression, anxiety, and bipolar II disorder. I've come to terms with the fact that they will be a part of me for the rest of my life because (and I say this reluctantly) they have made me into the woman I am today. And if overcoming these challenges require taking prescription drugs, doing yoga, writing, reading, going for walks, hanging out with friends even when I'm down, or even smoking a bit (okay, a lot) of weed, so be it. My mental ailments are now my friends, but what matters most is that I am now my own friend, and that is all I ever needed. Feel and enjoy!